Learning to Add

The **+** sign means you should **add**.

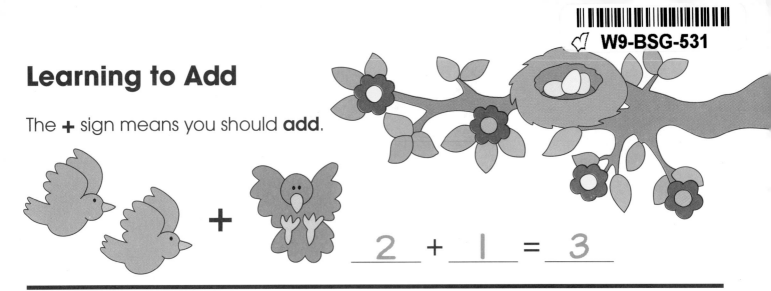

$$\underline{2} + \underline{1} = \underline{3}$$

The pictures below tell you to **add**. Read the story problem. Write the answer.

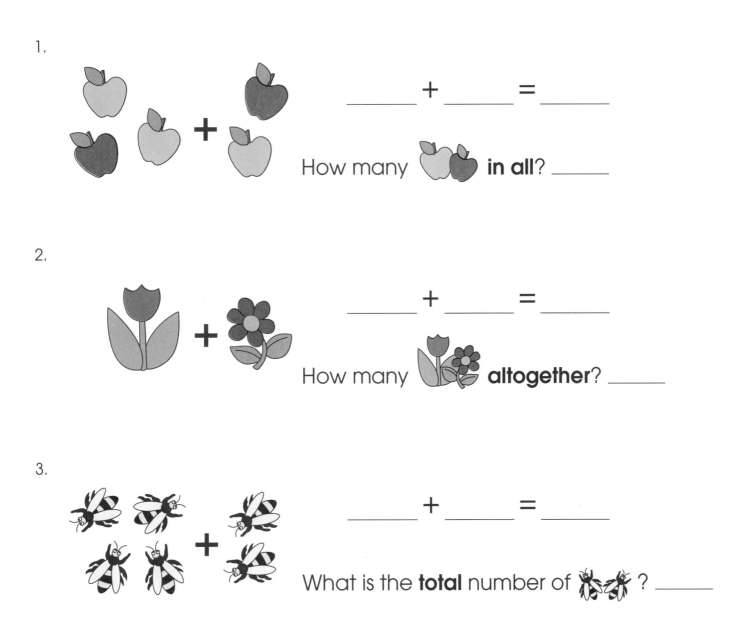

1.

_____ + _____ = _____

How many 🍎🍎 **in all**? _____

2.

_____ + _____ = _____

How many 🌷🌸 **altogether**? _____

3.

_____ + _____ = _____

What is the **total** number of 🐝🐝 ? _____

Addition Equations

$$\underline{}2\underline{} + \underline{}2\underline{} = \underline{}4\underline{}$$
in all

Read the story problem. Write the **equation**.

1.

_____ + _____ = _____
in all

2.

_____ + _____ = _____
in all

3.

_____ + _____ = _____
in all

Addition Problems

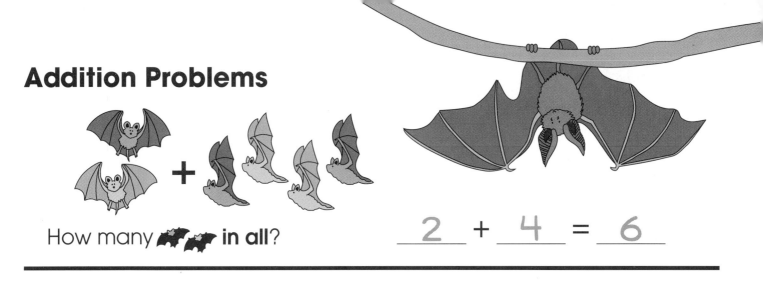

How many in all? $\underline{\ 2\ } + \underline{\ 4\ } = \underline{\ 6\ }$

Read the story problem. Write the **equation**.

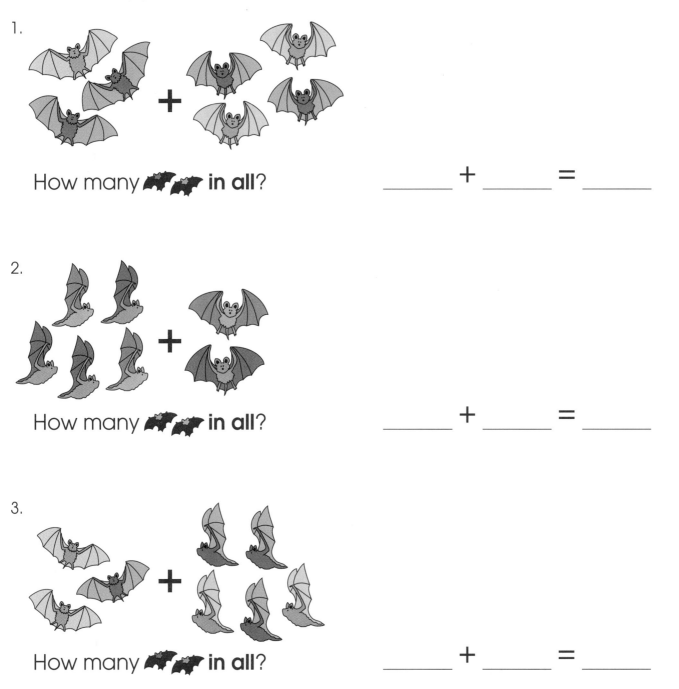

1.

How many bats in all?   _____ + _____ = _____

2.

How many bats in all?   _____ + _____ = _____

3.

How many bats in all?   _____ + _____ = _____

Wet Pets

How many  in all? __7__

$$3 + 4 = 7$$

Read the story problem. Write the answer.

1.

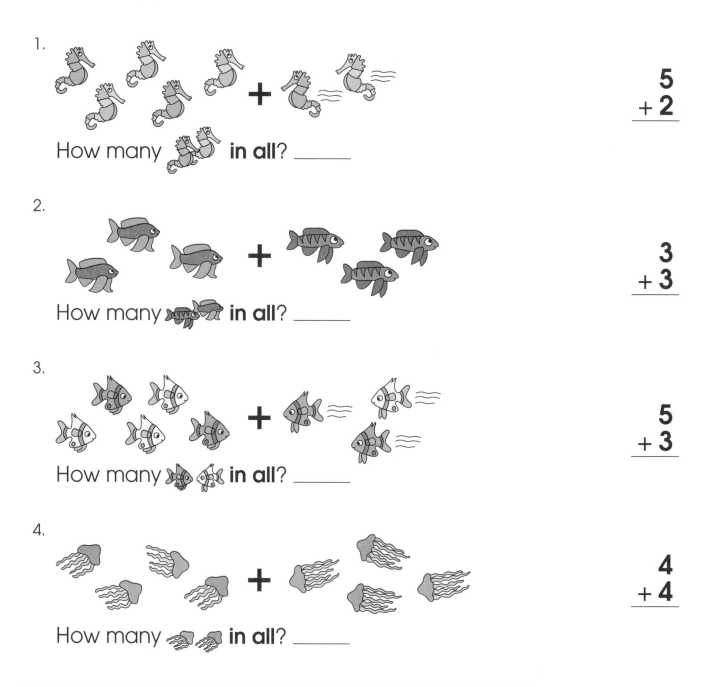

How many in all? _____

$$5 + 2$$

2.

How many in all? _____

$$3 + 3$$

3.

How many in all? _____

$$5 + 3$$

4.

How many in all? _____

$$4 + 4$$

Pets

Lisa has **3** fish.
Bill has **4** fish.
How many are there **in all**?

_____7_____ fish

$$\begin{array}{r} 3 \\ +\,4 \\ \hline 7 \end{array}$$

Read the story problem. Write the **equation**.

1. Hanna has **2** birds.
   Pat has **5** birds.
   How many are there **in all**?

   _____ birds

   _____
   _____
   _____

2. Jack saw **3** dogs.
   Then he saw **5** more.
   How many were there **in all**?

   _____ dogs

   _____
   _____
   _____

3. Abby has **2** kittens.
   Scott has **6** kittens.
   How many are there **in all**?

   _____ kittens

   _____
   _____
   _____

Pen Pals

Peter wrote **6** letters.
Tracy wrote **5** letters.
How many were there **in all**?

___11___ letters

$$\begin{array}{r} 6 \\ +\ 5 \\ \hline 11 \end{array}$$

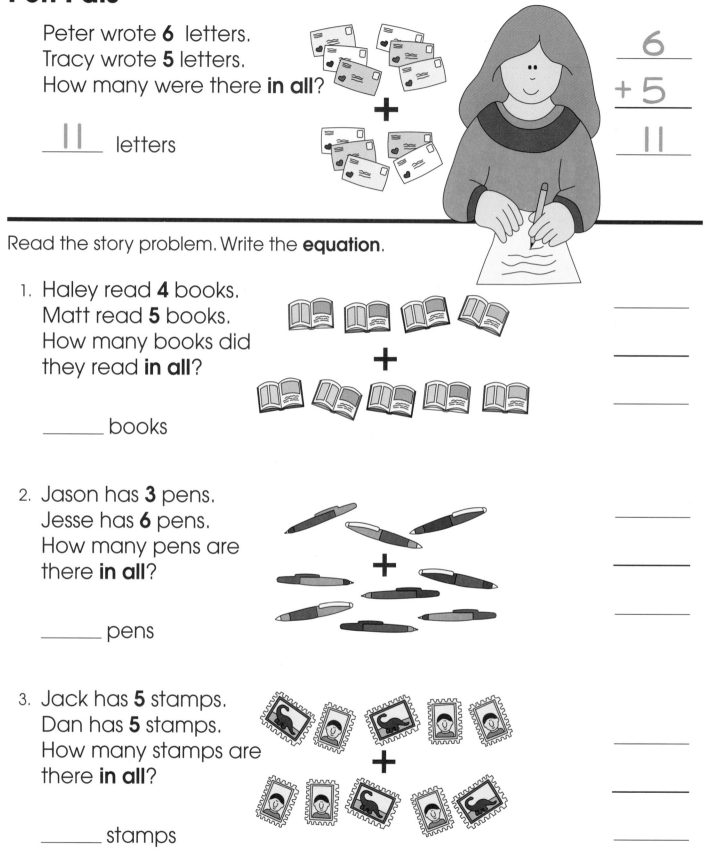

Read the story problem. Write the **equation**.

1. Haley read **4** books.
   Matt read **5** books.
   How many books did
   they read **in all**?

   _____ books

   _____
   _____
   _____

2. Jason has **3** pens.
   Jesse has **6** pens.
   How many pens are
   there **in all**?

   _____ pens

   _____
   _____
   _____

3. Jack has **5** stamps.
   Dan has **5** stamps.
   How many stamps are
   there **in all**?

   _____ stamps

   _____
   _____

Learning to Subtract

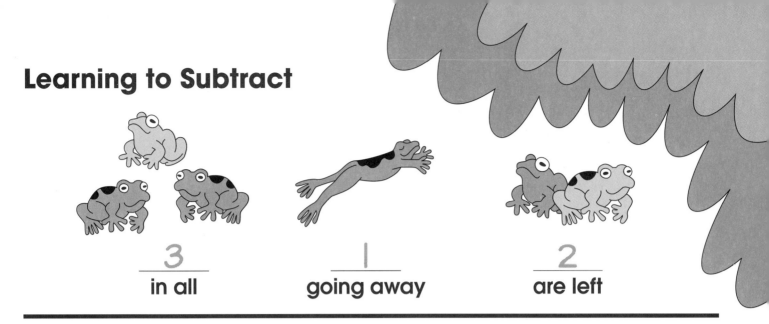

<u>3</u>

in all

<u>1</u>

going away

<u>2</u>

are left

Read the story problem. Write the number sentence. Find the answer.

1.

_____ **in all**

_____ **going away**

_____ **are left**

2.

_____ **in all**

_____ **going away**

_____ **are left**

3.

_____ **in all**

_____ **going away**

_____ **are left**

Subtraction Equations

The **–** sign means you should **subtract**.

_7_
_____
in all

_7_ – _3_ = _4_
_____   _____   _____
in all   are left

Read the story problem. Write the **equation**.

1.

_____
in all

_____ – _____ = _____
in all

2.

_____
in all

_____ – _____ = _____
in all

3.

_____
in all

_____ – _____ = _____
in all

Problem Solving

Read the story problem. Write the answer.

1. How many **are left**?

_____ frogs

2. How many **are left**?

_____ cats

3. How many **are left**?

_____ rabbits

4. How many **are left**?

_____ dogs

5. How many **are left**?

_____ mice

6. How many **are left**?

_____ birds

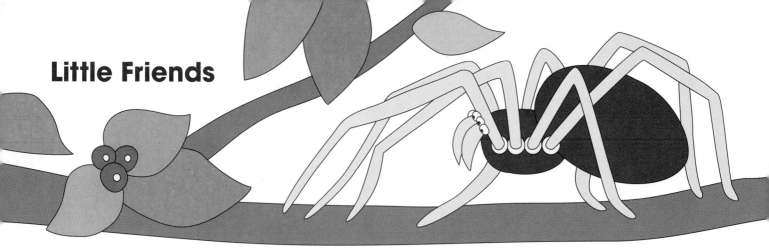

Little Friends

Read the story problem. Write the **equation**.

1.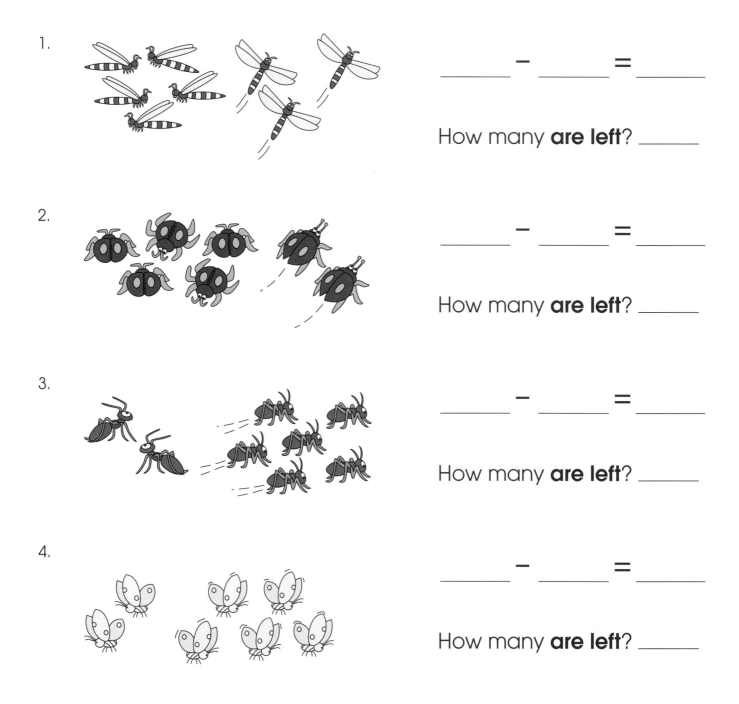

_____ – _____ = _____

How many **are left**? _____

2.

_____ – _____ = _____

How many **are left**? _____

3.

_____ – _____ = _____

How many **are left**? _____

4.

_____ – _____ = _____

How many **are left**? _____

Bees and Bears

6 bees were on a flower.
3 bees flew away.
How many bees were left?

_____3_____ bees

$$\begin{array}{r} 6 \\ -3 \\ \hline 3 \end{array}$$

Read the story problem. Write the **equation**.

1. **5** bees were at the hive.
   3 bees flew away.
   How many bees were left?

   _____ bees

   _____
   _____
   _____

2. **6** bears were in the woods.
   4 bears went away.
   How many bears were left?

   _____ bears

   _____
   _____
   _____

3. Bear had **6** jars of honey.
   He gave away **2**.
   How many jars of
   honey did he have left?

   _____ jars

   _____
   _____
   _____

Subtraction

Jim had **7** flowers.
He gave away **3** flowers.
How many did he have left?

$$\begin{array}{r} 7 \\ -\ 3 \\ \hline 4 \end{array}$$

__4__ flowers

Read the story problem. Write the **equation**.

1. Tiffany saw **8** birds.
   4 birds flew away.
   How many were left?

   _____ birds

   _____
   _____
   _____

2. Heidi had **6** apples.
   She ate **2** of them.
   How many did she have left?

   _____ apples

   _____
   _____
   _____

3. Tom found **8** shells.
   He broke **3** of them.
   How many did he have left?

   _____ shells

   _____
   _____
   _____

Add or Subtract

Christy had **7** oranges.
She bought **3** more.
How many does she have in all?

____10____ oranges

$$
\begin{array}{r}
7 \\
+\ 3 \\
\hline
10
\end{array}
$$

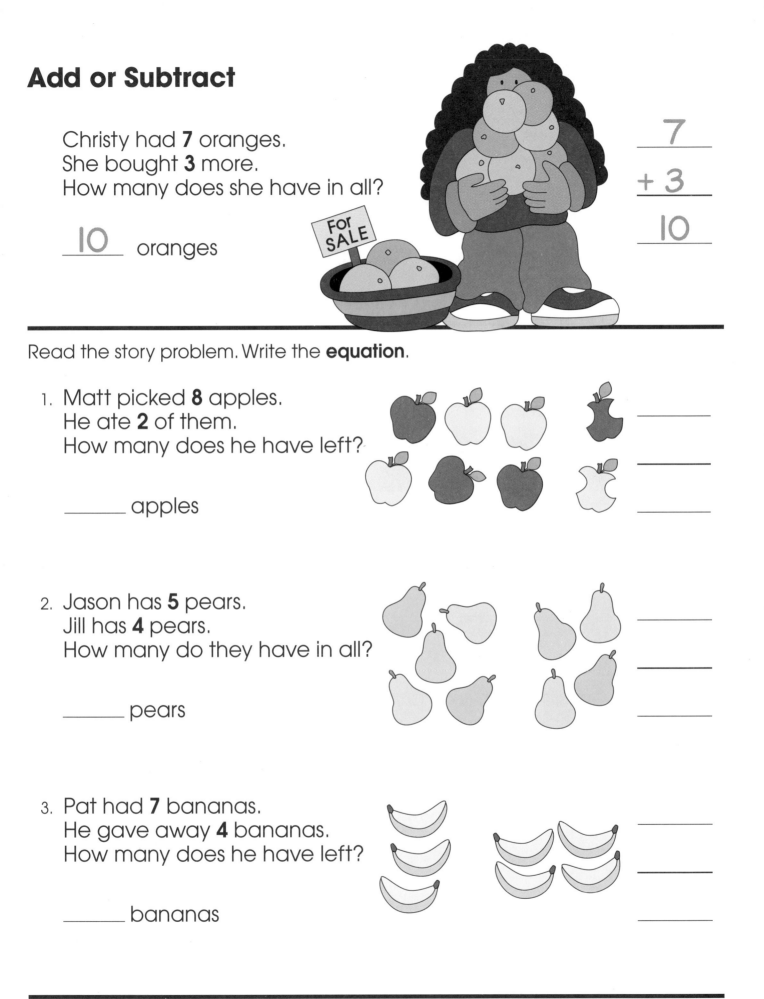

Read the story problem. Write the **equation**.

1. Matt picked **8** apples.
   He ate **2** of them.
   How many does he have left?

   _____ apples

   _____
   _____
   _____

2. Jason has **5** pears.
   Jill has **4** pears.
   How many do they have in all?

   _____ pears

   _____
   _____
   _____

3. Pat had **7** bananas.
   He gave away **4** bananas.
   How many does he have left?

   _____ bananas

   _____
   _____
   _____

Water Friends

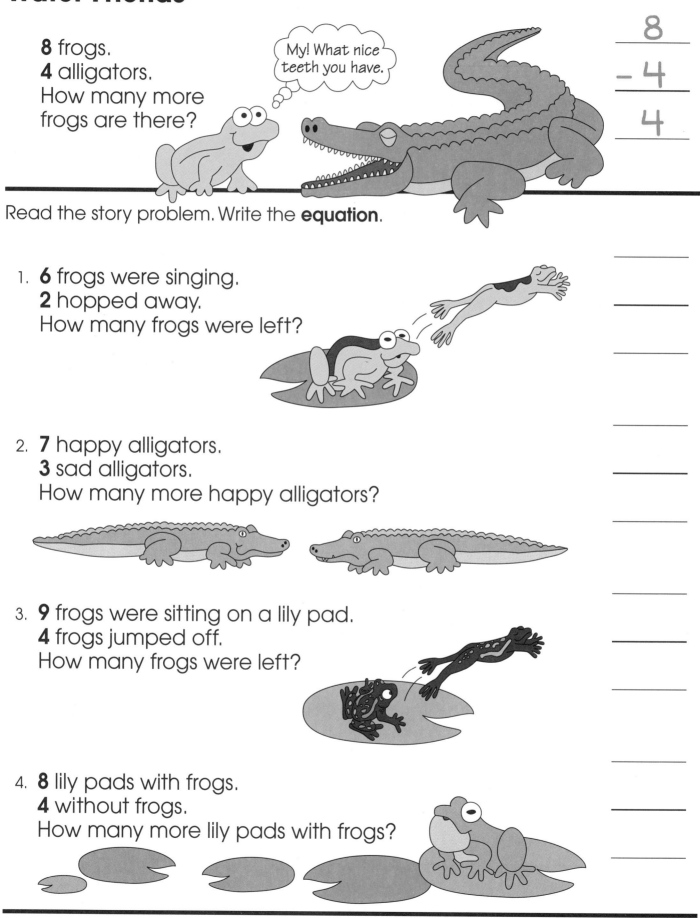

8 frogs.
4 alligators.
How many more
frogs are there?

My! What nice teeth you have.

$$\begin{array}{r} 8 \\ -4 \\ \hline 4 \end{array}$$

Read the story problem. Write the **equation**.

1. **6** frogs were singing.
   2 hopped away.
   How many frogs were left?

2. **7** happy alligators.
   3 sad alligators.
   How many more happy alligators?

3. **9** frogs were sitting on a lily pad.
   4 frogs jumped off.
   How many frogs were left?

4. **8** lily pads with frogs.
   4 without frogs.
   How many more lily pads with frogs?

Picture Graphs and Story Problems

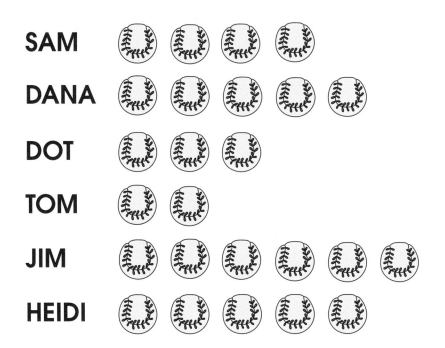

SAM

DANA

DOT

TOM

JIM

HEIDI

1. How many baseballs does Sam have? _____

2. How many does Dana have? _____

3. How many does Dot have? _____

4. How many does Tom have? _____

5. How many does Jim have? _____

6. How many does Heidi have? _____

7. How many baseballs do Dot and Dana have altogether?

   _____ ☐ _____ = _____

8. Jim has more baseballs than Sam.
   How many more baseballs does Jim have?

   _____ ☐ _____ = _____

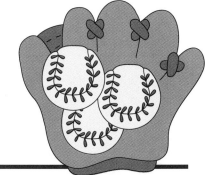

Picture Graphs and Story Problems

CAROL	ANN	NICK	PETE	LISA	DAN

1. How many pets does Dan have? _____

2. How many pets does Ann have? _____

3. How many pets does Lisa have? _____

4. How many pets does Nick have? _____

5. How many pets do Carol and Pete have in all?

   _____ ☐ _____ = _____

6. Nick has more pets than Dan.
   How many more pets does Nick have?

   _____ ☐ _____ = _____

Bar Graphs and Story Problems

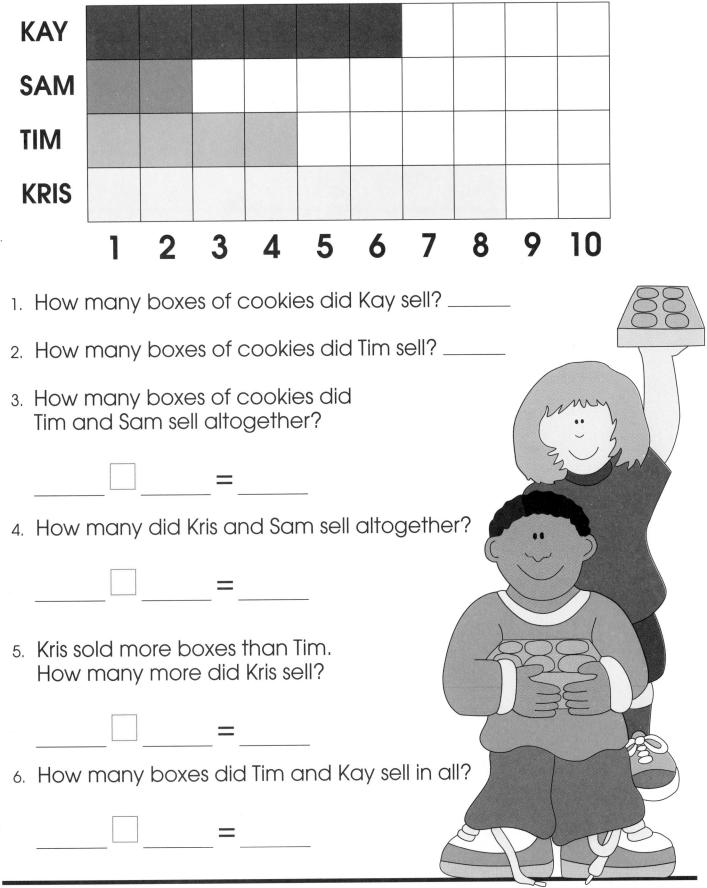

	1	2	3	4	5	6	7	8	9	10
KAY	■	■	■	■	■	■				
SAM	■	■								
TIM	■	■	■	■						
KRIS	■	■	■	■	■	■	■	■		

1. How many boxes of cookies did Kay sell? _____

2. How many boxes of cookies did Tim sell? _____

3. How many boxes of cookies did
   Tim and Sam sell altogether?

   _____ ☐ _____ = _____

4. How many did Kris and Sam sell altogether?

   _____ ☐ _____ = _____

5. Kris sold more boxes than Tim.
   How many more did Kris sell?

   _____ ☐ _____ = _____

6. How many boxes did Tim and Kay sell in all?

   _____ ☐ _____ = _____

Bar Graphs and Story Problems

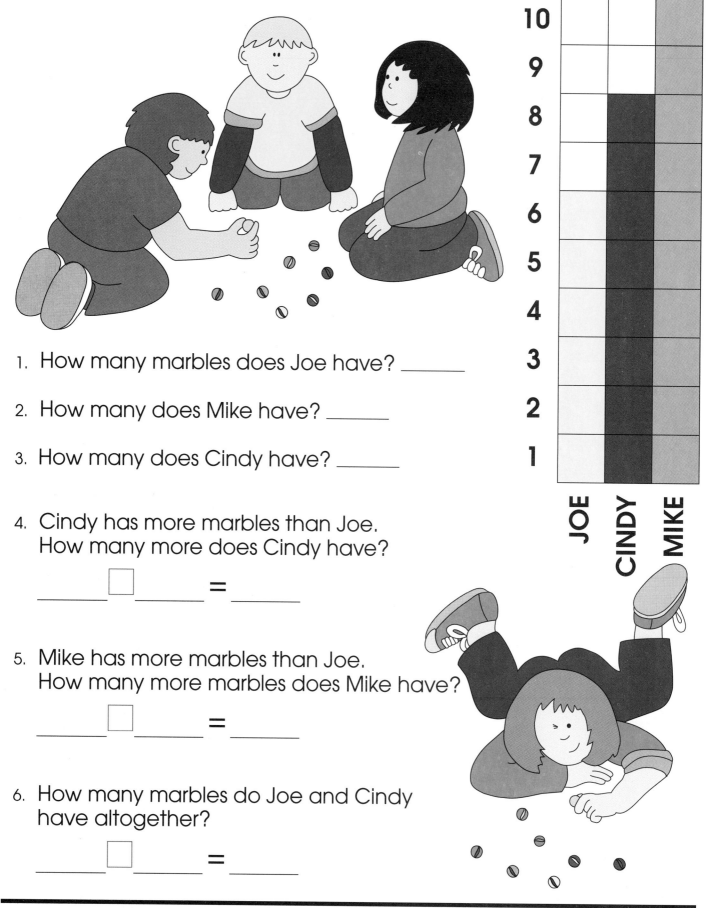

10			
9			
8			
7			
6			
5			
4			
3			
2			
1			
	JOE	CINDY	MIKE

1. How many marbles does Joe have? _____

2. How many does Mike have? _____

3. How many does Cindy have? _____

4. Cindy has more marbles than Joe. How many more does Cindy have?

   _____ ☐ _____ = _____

5. Mike has more marbles than Joe. How many more marbles does Mike have?

   _____ ☐ _____ = _____

6. How many marbles do Joe and Cindy have altogether?

   _____ ☐ _____ = _____

Problem Solving

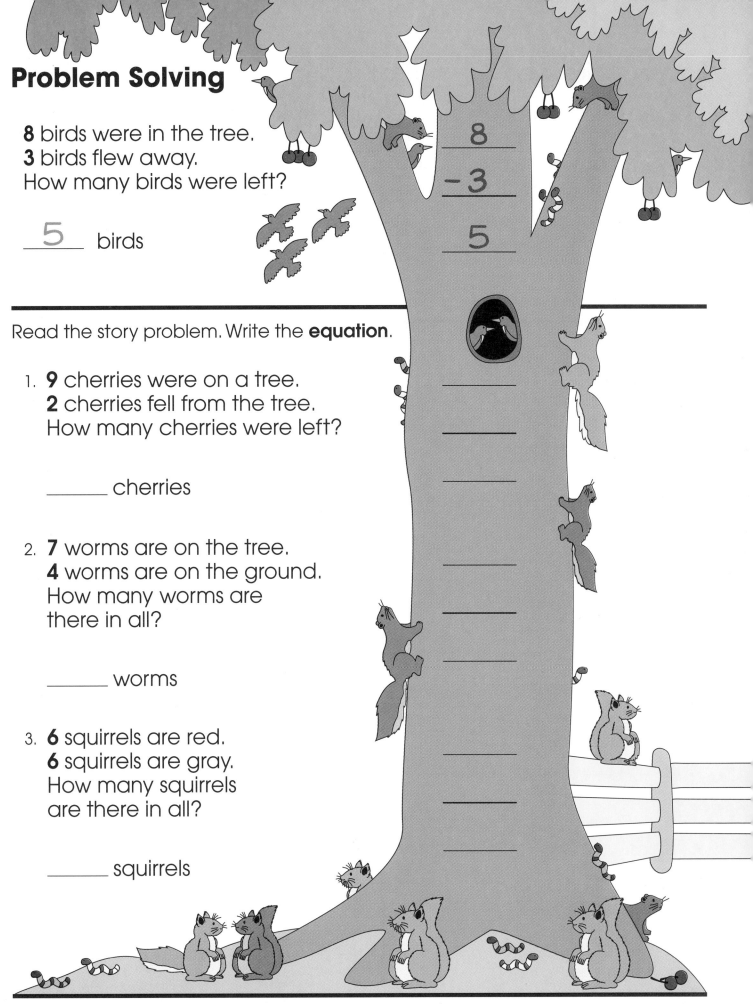

8 birds were in the tree.
3 birds flew away.
How many birds were left?

___5___ birds

$$\begin{array}{r} 8 \\ -3 \\ \hline 5 \end{array}$$

Read the story problem. Write the **equation**.

1. **9** cherries were on a tree.
    2 cherries fell from the tree.
    How many cherries were left?

    _____ cherries

2. **7** worms are on the tree.
    4 worms are on the ground.
    How many worms are
    there in all?

    _____ worms

3. **6** squirrels are red.
    6 squirrels are gray.
    How many squirrels
    are there in all?

    _____ squirrels

Loose Change

David has **5** quarters.
Nora has **5** quarters.
How many quarters
are there in all?

$$
\begin{array}{r}
5 \\
+\ 5 \\
\hline
10
\end{array}
$$

___10___ quarters

Read the story problem. Write the **equation**.

1. Alex had **9** pennies.
   He gave **4** away.
   How many pennies
   does he have now?

   _____ pennies

   _____

   _____

   _____

2. Wendy has **4** nickels.
   Jim has **3**. Jon has **6**.
   How many nickels are
   there in all?

   _____ nickels

   _____

   _____

   _____

3. Kate had **9** dimes.
   She spent **3**.
   How many dimes
   does she have left?

   _____ dimes

   _____

   _____

   _____

Let's Have a Party

Deb had **6** party hats.
She found **5** more.
How many does she
have in all?

___||___ party hats

$$\begin{array}{r} 6 \\ +\,5 \\ \hline 11 \end{array}$$

Read the story problem. Write the **equation**.

1. Randy has **11** presents.
He unwrapped **4** presents.
How many does he have
left to unwrap?

_____ presents

_____

_____

_____

2. Tina had **10** balloons.
She gave away **7** of them.
How many balloons does
she have now?

_____ balloons

_____

_____

_____

3. Mike counted **11** cupcakes.
Then he counted **4** more.
How many are there in all?

_____ cupcakes

_____

_____

_____

Garden Friends

Write an **equation** for each story problem.

1. There were **10** ladybugs in the garden.
   5 ladybugs left.

   _____
   _____
   _____

2. **11** beetles were on a log.
   3 more came along.

   _____
   _____
   _____

3. **8** ants were on the watermelon.
   7 more were on the ground.

   _____
   _____
   _____

4. **12** bees were at the hive.
   3 flew away.

   _____
   _____
   _____

Down on the Farm

11 roosters were on a fence.
5 jumped off.
How many roosters were left?

<u> 6 </u> roosters

$$\begin{array}{r} 11 \\ -5 \\ \hline 6 \end{array}$$

Write an **equation** for each story problem.

1. **7** hens were in the pen.
   5 hens were in the yard.
   How many were there in all?

   _____ hens

   _____
   _____
   _____

2. **8** chicks were white.
   5 chicks were black.
   How many chicks
   were there in all?

   _____ chicks

   _____
   _____
   _____

3. **12** eggs were in the nest.
   4 hatched.
   How many eggs were left?

   _____ eggs

   _____
   _____
   _____

Summertime

Jerry had **11** cherries.
He ate **3** of them.
How many does he
have now?

___8___ cherries

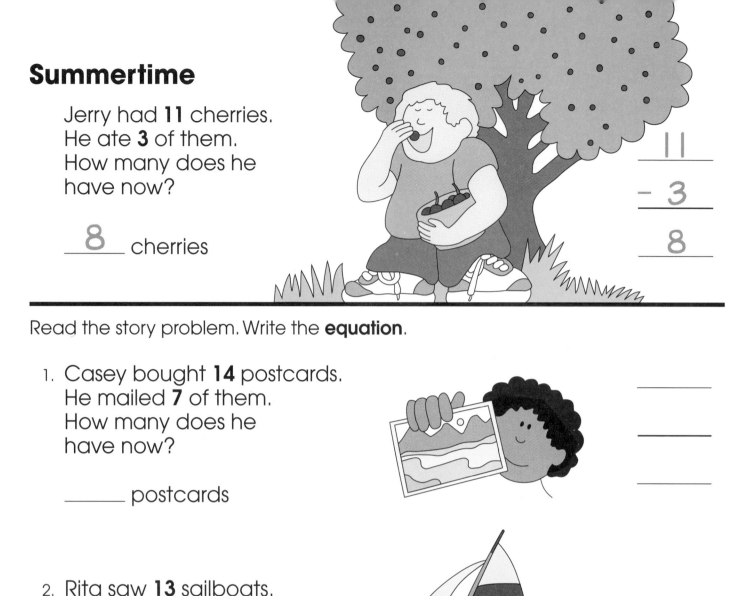

$$\begin{array}{r} 11 \\ -\ 3 \\ \hline 8 \end{array}$$

Read the story problem. Write the **equation**.

1. Casey bought **14** postcards.
   He mailed **7** of them.
   How many does he
   have now?

   _____ postcards

   _____
   _____

2. Rita saw **13** sailboats.
   Then she saw **6** more sailboats.
   How many sailboats did
   Rita see in all?

   _____ sailboats

   _____
   _____

3. Robin caught **15** fish.
   8 fish got away.
   How many does she
   have now?

   _____ fish

   _____
   _____

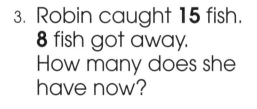

At the Beach

Tina saw **7** beach balls.
Then she saw **5** more.
How many beach balls
did Tina see altogether?

_12_ beach balls

$$
\begin{array}{r}
7 \\
+ 5 \\
\hline
12
\end{array}
$$

Read the story problem. Write the **equation**.

1. Brian had **16** fishhooks.
   He lost **4** of them.
   How many fishhooks
   does he have left?

   _____ fishhooks

2. Mandy took **13** pictures.
   Then she took **5** more pictures.
   How many did she take in all?

   _____ pictures

3. Jan found **12** shells.
   7 shells broke.
   How many shells does
   she have left?

   _____ shells

Signs of Spring

Barry saw **16** ladybugs.
8 flew away.
How many were left?

_____8_____ ladybugs

16
− 8
‾‾‾‾
8

Read the story problem. Write the **equation**.

1. Maggie saw **13** tulips at school.
   She saw **11** more at home.
   How many did she see in all?

   _____ tulips

   _____
   _____
   _____

2. Haley had **23** plants.
   She bought **14** more plants.
   How many were there in all?

   _____ plants

   _____
   _____
   _____

3. Luis saw **34** butterflies.
   13 flew away.
   How many were left?

   _____ butterflies

   _____
   _____
   _____

4. Karla had **25¢**.
   She spent **15¢** for seeds.
   How much did she have left?

   _____ ¢

   _____ ¢
   _____ ¢
   _____ ¢

Springtime Fun

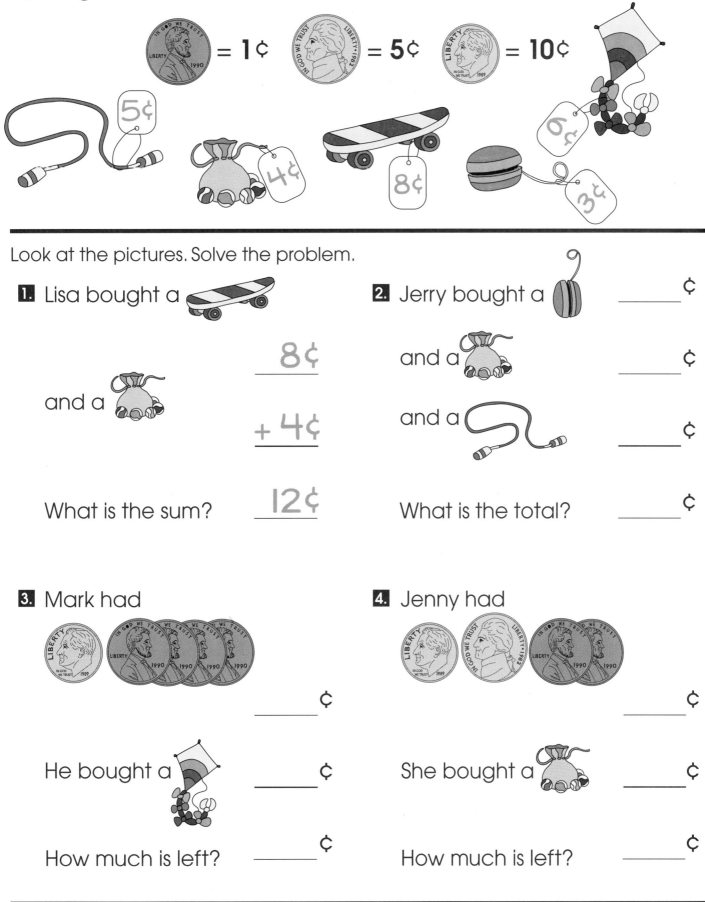

Look at the pictures. Solve the problem.

1. Lisa bought a

and a

8¢

+ 4¢

What is the sum?   12¢

2. Jerry bought a _____ ¢

and a _____ ¢

and a _____ ¢

What is the total?   _____ ¢

3. Mark had

_____ ¢

He bought a _____ ¢

How much is left?   _____ ¢

4. Jenny had

_____ ¢

She bought a _____ ¢

How much is left?   _____ ¢

At the Ballpark

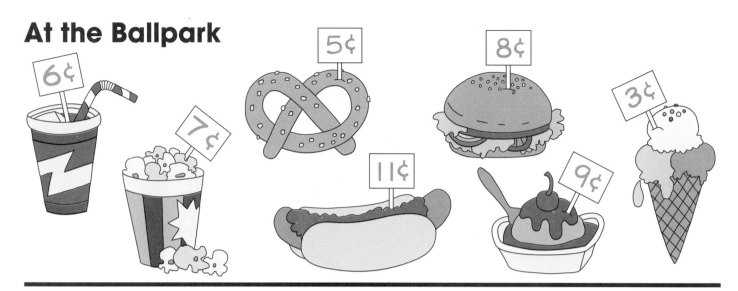

Read the story problem. Write the **equation**.

1. Jackie had **48¢**

She bought a

How much did she have left?

$$48¢$$
$$- \ 6¢$$
$$42¢$$

2. Jim bought a

and a

How much did he spend?

_____
_____
_____

3. Jan bought

and a

How much did she spend?

_____
_____
_____

4. Marcie had **15¢**

She bought a

How much did she have left?

_____
_____
_____

5. Ted bought a

and a

How much did he spend?

_____
_____
_____

6. Rich had **12¢**

He bought

How much did he have left?

_____
_____
_____

Hobbies

Read the story problem. Write the **equation**.

1. Haley collects old coins.
   She has **37** old nickels and
   43 old pennies. How many more
   pennies than nickels does she have?

   _____
   _____
   _____

2. Peter collects stamps.
   He has **29** United States stamps.
   34 stamps are from other countries.
   How many stamps does he
   have in all?

   _____
   _____
   _____

3. Hanna collects buttons.
   She has **58** in her collection.
   Her aunt sent her **18** more.
   How many buttons does she
   have altogether?

   _____
   _____

4. Juan and Maria collect wildflowers.
   Juan has **38** in his collection.
   Maria has **56**. How many more
   wildflowers does Maria
   have than Juan?

   _____
   _____

Solving Story Problems

Read the story problem. Write the **equation**.

1. **129** children attend Hawthorn School. **148** attend Henry School. How many more children go to Henry School?

   _____

   _____

   _____

2. There were **138** adults at the game. There were **126** children. How many people were at the game altogether?

   _____

   _____

3. The Jays scored **79** points during the game. The Tigers scored **87**. How many more points did the Tigers score?

   _____

   _____

4. **116** hot dogs with mustard were sold. **118** hot dogs with ketchup were sold. How many hot dogs were sold altogether?

   _____

   _____

Answer Key

Page 1
1. 3 + 2 = 5
2. 1 + 1 = 2
3. 4 + 2 = 6

Page 2
1. 3 + 3 = 6
2. 4 + 2 = 6
3. 5 + 1 = 6

Page 3
1. 3 + 4 = 7
2. 5 + 2 = 7
3. 3 + 5 = 8

Page 4
1. 7
2. 6
3. 8
4. 8

Page 5
1. 7 birds, $\begin{array}{r} 2 \\ +\,5 \\ \hline 7 \end{array}$
2. 8 dogs, $\begin{array}{r} 3 \\ +\,5 \\ \hline 8 \end{array}$
3. 8 kittens, $\begin{array}{r} 2 \\ +\,6 \\ \hline 8 \end{array}$

Page 6
1. 9 books, $\begin{array}{r} 4 \\ +\,5 \\ \hline 9 \end{array}$
2. 9 pens, $\begin{array}{r} 3 \\ +\,6 \\ \hline 9 \end{array}$
3. 10 stamps, $\begin{array}{r} 5 \\ +\,5 \\ \hline 10 \end{array}$

Page 7
1. 4, 2, 2
2. 5, 3, 2
3. 6, 4, 2

Page 8
1. 6, 6 − 1 = 5
2. 6, 6 − 4 = 2
3. 5, 5 − 3 = 2

Page 9
1. 3   2. 2
3. 4   4. 4
5. 2   6. 3

Page 10
1. 8 − 3 = 5, 5
2. 7 − 2 = 5, 5
3. 8 − 6 = 2, 2
4. 7 − 5 = 2, 2

Page 11
1. 2 bees, $\begin{array}{r} 5 \\ -\,3 \\ \hline 2 \end{array}$
2. 2 bears, $\begin{array}{r} 6 \\ -\,4 \\ \hline 2 \end{array}$
3. 4 jars, $\begin{array}{r} 6 \\ -\,2 \\ \hline 4 \end{array}$

Page 12
1. 4 birds, $\begin{array}{r} 8 \\ -\,4 \\ \hline 4 \end{array}$
2. 4 apples, $\begin{array}{r} 6 \\ -\,2 \\ \hline 4 \end{array}$
3. 5 shells, $\begin{array}{r} 8 \\ -\,3 \\ \hline 5 \end{array}$

Page 13
1. 6 apples, $\begin{array}{r} 8 \\ -\,2 \\ \hline 6 \end{array}$
2. 9 pears, $\begin{array}{r} 5 \\ +\,4 \\ \hline 9 \end{array}$
3. 3 bananas, $\begin{array}{r} 7 \\ -\,4 \\ \hline 3 \end{array}$

Page 14
1. $\begin{array}{r} 6 \\ -\,2 \\ \hline 4 \end{array}$
2. $\begin{array}{r} 7 \\ -\,3 \\ \hline 4 \end{array}$
3. $\begin{array}{r} 9 \\ -\,4 \\ \hline 5 \end{array}$
4. $\begin{array}{r} 8 \\ -\,4 \\ \hline 4 \end{array}$

Page 15
1. 4
2. 5
3. 3
4. 2
5. 6
6. 5
7. 3 + 5 = 8
8. 6 − 4 = 2

Page 16
1. 5
2. 3
3. 2
4. 7
5. 2 + 4 = 6
6. 7 − 5 = 2

Page 17
1. 6
2. 4
3. 4 + 2 = 6
4. 8 + 2 = 10
5. 8 − 4 = 4
6. 4 + 6 = 10

Answer Key

Page 18
1. 6
2. 10
3. 8
4. 8 − 6 = 2
5. 10 − 6 = 4
6. 6 + 8 = 14

Page 19
1. 7 cherries,
$$\begin{array}{r} 9 \\ -2 \\ \hline 7 \end{array}$$
2. 11 worms,
$$\begin{array}{r} 7 \\ +4 \\ \hline 11 \end{array}$$
3. 12 squirrels,
$$\begin{array}{r} 6 \\ +6 \\ \hline 12 \end{array}$$

Page 20
1. 5 pennies,
$$\begin{array}{r} 9 \\ -4 \\ \hline 5 \end{array}$$
2. 13 nickels,
$$\begin{array}{r} 4 \\ 3 \\ +6 \\ \hline 13 \end{array}$$
3. 6 dimes,
$$\begin{array}{r} 9 \\ -3 \\ \hline 6 \end{array}$$

Page 21
1. 7 presents,
$$\begin{array}{r} 11 \\ -4 \\ \hline 7 \end{array}$$
2. 3 balloons,
$$\begin{array}{r} 10 \\ -7 \\ \hline 3 \end{array}$$
3. 15 cupcakes,
$$\begin{array}{r} 11 \\ +4 \\ \hline 15 \end{array}$$

Page 22
1.
$$\begin{array}{r} 10 \\ -5 \\ \hline 5 \end{array}$$
2.
$$\begin{array}{r} 11 \\ +3 \\ \hline 14 \end{array}$$
3.
$$\begin{array}{r} 8 \\ +7 \\ \hline 15 \end{array}$$
4.
$$\begin{array}{r} 12 \\ -3 \\ \hline 9 \end{array}$$

Page 23
1. 12 hens,
$$\begin{array}{r} 7 \\ +5 \\ \hline 12 \end{array}$$
2. 13 chicks,
$$\begin{array}{r} 8 \\ +5 \\ \hline 13 \end{array}$$
3. 8 eggs,
$$\begin{array}{r} 12 \\ -4 \\ \hline 8 \end{array}$$

Page 24
1. 7 postcards,
$$\begin{array}{r} 14 \\ -7 \\ \hline 7 \end{array}$$
2. 19 sailboats,
$$\begin{array}{r} 13 \\ +6 \\ \hline 19 \end{array}$$
3. 7 fish,
$$\begin{array}{r} 15 \\ -8 \\ \hline 7 \end{array}$$

Page 25
1. 12 fishhooks,
$$\begin{array}{r} 16 \\ -4 \\ \hline 12 \end{array}$$
2. 18 pictures,
$$\begin{array}{r} 13 \\ +5 \\ \hline 18 \end{array}$$
3. 5 shells,
$$\begin{array}{r} 12 \\ -7 \\ \hline 5 \end{array}$$

Page 26
1. 24 tulips,
$$\begin{array}{r} 13 \\ +11 \\ \hline 24 \end{array}$$
2. 37 plants,
$$\begin{array}{r} 23 \\ +14 \\ \hline 37 \end{array}$$
3. 21 butterflies,
$$\begin{array}{r} 34 \\ -13 \\ \hline 21 \end{array}$$
4. 10¢,
$$\begin{array}{r} 25¢ \\ -15¢ \\ \hline 10¢ \end{array}$$

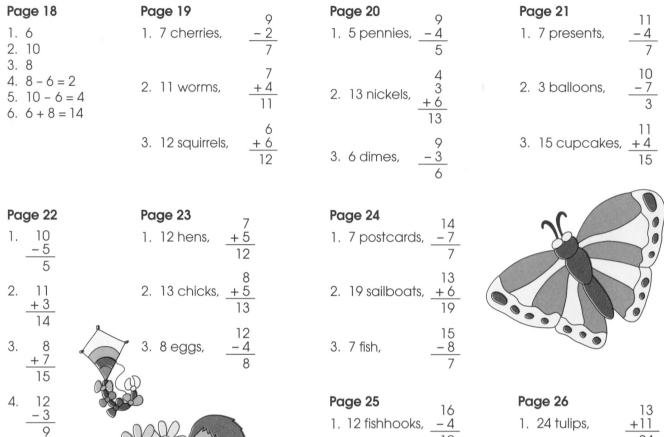

Page 27
1.
$$\begin{array}{r} 8¢ \\ +4¢ \\ \hline 12¢ \end{array}$$
2.
$$\begin{array}{r} 3¢ \\ 4¢ \\ +5¢ \\ \hline 12¢ \end{array}$$
3.
$$\begin{array}{r} 14¢ \\ -6¢ \\ \hline 8¢ \end{array}$$
4.
$$\begin{array}{r} 17¢ \\ -4¢ \\ \hline 13¢ \end{array}$$

Page 28
1.
$$\begin{array}{r} 48¢ \\ -6¢ \\ \hline 42¢ \end{array}$$
2.
$$\begin{array}{r} 11¢ \\ +8¢ \\ \hline 19¢ \end{array}$$
3.
$$\begin{array}{r} 7¢ \\ +9¢ \\ \hline 16¢ \end{array}$$
4.
$$\begin{array}{r} 15¢ \\ -3¢ \\ \hline 12¢ \end{array}$$
5.
$$\begin{array}{r} 6¢ \\ +5¢ \\ \hline 11¢ \end{array}$$
6.
$$\begin{array}{r} 12¢ \\ -7¢ \\ \hline 5¢ \end{array}$$

Page 29
1.
$$\begin{array}{r} 43 \\ -37 \\ \hline 6 \end{array}$$
2.
$$\begin{array}{r} 29 \\ +34 \\ \hline 63 \end{array}$$
3.
$$\begin{array}{r} 58 \\ +18 \\ \hline 76 \end{array}$$
4.
$$\begin{array}{r} 56 \\ -38 \\ \hline 18 \end{array}$$

Page 30
1.
$$\begin{array}{r} 148 \\ -129 \\ \hline 19 \end{array}$$
2.
$$\begin{array}{r} 138 \\ +126 \\ \hline 264 \end{array}$$
3.
$$\begin{array}{r} 87 \\ -79 \\ \hline 8 \end{array}$$
4.
$$\begin{array}{r} 116 \\ +118 \\ \hline 234 \end{array}$$